THE POCKET GUIDE TO PLOTTING

TROY LAMBERT

by Troy Lambert
© Copyright 2023, All Rights Reserved
The information in this book is for general instructional purposes only, and you must apply what is shared here to your own unique writing and your situation. While every endeavor has been made to make sure the information is correct, the application is up to each individual.

That being said, we hope the information contained herein is helpful to your author journey. However, no part of this book may be copied, shared, or distributed for any purpose without the express written permission of the author and/or the publisher. Doing so is not only illegal, it's just bad juju.

CONTENTS

INTRODUCTION

I wrote this book for one reason: to answer a question a lot of people ask me when they want to write a book: Where do I start? The answer is always more complex than they initially thought.

You may have noted by the cover and the reference to the dude above that I am a fan of *The Big Lebowski*. It's a cult classic with an obscure plot, but it has some elements we will talk about later that make it a great story: interesting people in interesting places doing interesting things, and doing them in an interesting way.

So if this book sometimes sounds like I wrote it when drinking White Russians (a Caucasian, according to The Dude) and watching too much Big Lebowski—well, that might be on purpose.

Because while it is nice to have an idea for a story (I have lots of them, if you want to steal a few), but developing it into a narrative, one that will be long enough for a novel or even a novella is something different altogether. I am assuming a couple things if you downloaded this book.

I assume you have a story you want to tell. I also assume you want to tell it in writing, in some kind of written format. What do I mean by that?

I'll give you an example. A memoir is a story. It's mostly true from your point of view (although others in your life might disagree) but it still needs to have a story arc, character development, a theme, and a premise that a reader will want to know more about. Otherwise, it is just a series of events that have happened in your life. Even your kids don't want to hear you tell those stories again, or at least mine don't want to hear them after the number of tellings reaches the teens. Besides that, your life will never be made into a movie, and the star you think you most resemble will never play you.

In addition, ladies, Jason Mamola, or whoever your favorite male star is, will not play your husband. A script for a movie is also a story. Each television episode is a story within a season, each season a story within the series, and so on. Sermons on Sunday are made up of stories, as are political speeches and sales pitches.

But is everything really a story? Well, it should be.

WHAT ABOUT NON-FICTION INSTRUCTIONAL OR INSPIRATIONAL BOOKS

Even non-fiction instructional or inspirational books are stories: the present the reader with a problem, a pain point. Then you describe the problem and present the obstacles or challenges the reader might face as a result. In general, the pain points you present should each get more challenging, causing the reader to react with things like, "Yep, that is true" and "I do struggle with that." This is the reactive section of your book. The reader is reacting to what you have told them and how these examples align with their experiences.

This happens until the midpoint of your book, which is when you present them with your solution, and how it addresses each pain point. This results in your hero (which in this case is your reader) becoming pro-active. You show them that by implementing the solutions you have outlined for them, they can become their own hero, and solve the problem or challenge they are facing. Your advice becomes a weapon, provided by you, the mentor, to defeat a powerful enemy,

In any case, assuming you want to write a any kind of story, when you ask, "Where do I start?" the answer is with a plot or an outline. You need to give your skeleton of an idea some bone structure, so you know what it is. A pile of bones could be nearly anything. Until you arrange them in the proper order, you have no idea what they represent.

It's also like a recipe: at some point you need to assemble all of your ingredients and then put them together. But in many cases, if you are baking a cake and mix things in the wrong order or cook it at the wrong temperature, it won't turn out right.

And your readers will tell you so. They may not know what is wrong, but they will recognize that something is not right. If your cake is raw in the middle or you forgot the sugar, it simply won't taste good, and people will not want to eat it. Either that, or they will chew politely and throw it away (or feed it to the dog) when you are not looking.

Of course, there are different ways of assembling the ingredients or the parts to your book, and we need to address one of those right away.

THE DISCOVERY WRITER

Some writers are discovery writers and write "into the dark" to discover the plot as they go. That is actually fine. You will still plot at some point.

This is because you have really written a zero draft or even what I call an outline draft. You have told yourself the story, and therefore assembled your ingredients. But the sooner you can apply a structure to them, even in a small way, the fewer drafts you will have to write.

That's because plotting is all about efficiency. It helps even discovery writers spot plot holes, extra scenes, and other issues before your second draft. But like other things, there are degrees of being a discovery writer, and most "pantsers" as discovery writers are often called, fall into one of four categories.

After the Draft

First, you can use the tools outlined in this book after you have written your first draft to help you with the re-writing and revision process. The way it works is this: you'll take each scene in your draft and summarize it. This gives you distance from your story. We'll explore that in a later volume completely dedicated to revision.

You'll be able to look at your story skeleton then, and see if you have any critical bones missing, like a femur or something, and you will also be able to see if you have added any extra limbs.

Perhaps my mystery and thriller writer is showing, and you prefer another analogy like the pieces of a puzzle, the rungs on a long, tall ladder you want to climb, or the ingredients to a carrot cake (In case you ever want to send me cake). Whatever that analogy is, the meaning is the same.

If something is missing, broken, or in the wrong place, you'll be able to identify it, and unlike your cake that has already been baked, fix it before anyone takes a bite.

Usually these writers create faster second drafts and increase their productivity by applying some sort of plot structure soon after the first draft is complete. But for some writers this does not work.

Plot as You Go

This is sometimes called the cycle method and is the one used by Dean Wesley Smith and other authors. This is when you write something one day, the next day you read it, and then continue the story where you left off. The next day, you repeat that process, and so on, ending up with a pretty polished draft, and usually one where you eventually figured out where you were going at some point along the way.

It's perfectly valid, but I would encourage you to add an extra layer of organization by summarizing what you have written each day, and the next day read the summary instead of the entire text you have written. It will speed the process, and again will give you distance from your own writing.

Then you will have less to re-read in each day, and at the end of your first draft you will have...

An outline of what you have written.

Then you can use that to revise as needed. Your second draft, can be completed much faster, improving both your stories and your productivity.

Tentpole Plotting

A tentpole plot is one where you, the writer, know four or five key events in the story, and you discovery write between those points. For example:

- You might know the inciting incident is where your characters meet in a romance.
- You may know the reasons that drive them apart and cause the central conflict in your story.
- You may know the darkest moment in your story when it appears they will never reunite.
- You may know how they get back together, and the ending.

Of course this is for a romance. In the case of mysteries, you might want to know who gets killed, who kills them, how the victim is killed, how they get caught, and maybe a few other details that will help you know how to leave clues along the way, and gives you a destination for your story.

Of course, none of this is essential to writing a story, aa the next type of plotter shows.

Plot, what Plot?

Some writers are still resistant to any plotting, as they feel it hampers their creativity. That is understandable as well, but some of them instead use a loose plot to keep track of things like the description of their characters, settings, and other story details. They don't plot per se, but they do track elements of their stories so they can refer to them as they go along.

This can be called a story bible, and in the case of a series of books, a series bible. This is useful no matter what kind of plotting you do, and we'll talk more about it later in this guide.

Of course, if you are a plotter and outliner, you already understand this process. You may outline in a very detailed way, or you may start with fewer pieces in place, but typically you will have some of the basest elements of the story outlined in some manner before you begin. So what are the elements that make a good story?

WHAT MAKES A GOOD STORY?

Let's start with a simple story format before we go deeper. A story, according to Dean Wesley Smith, is an interesting character in an interesting place doing interesting things in an interesting way. Let's tear that apart a bit, and then we are going to use that definition to build our plotting process.

Let's look at the fact that the word "interesting' describes every single part of this process. If something is not interesting, why do we want to read about it? We don't. Most of us, despite our best efforts or because of them, lead pretty uninteresting lives. Why?

Because what makes something interesting is conflict or danger, and most of us want to avoid both of those things on a regular basis. For example, you might want to solo climb El Capitan and write a book about it, and then have someone make a movie since someone filmed you doing it. However, you wouldn't want to do that every day. Even an adrenaline junkie needs a break between risks.

Even those who take risks every day find a way to cope which establishes risk as a part of their normal. Think stockbrokers or pretty much any small business owner including freelance writers. Every day there is the risk that what you do, what you write, or the stocks you pick will go south. You may lose money and lose enough of it and you will go broke. That risk usually has a countering payoff, but that type of risk is somewhat normalized. We don't even want to read about that day to day worry, what we want to read about is extraordinary conflict that breaks routine.

When you consider those who face much higher stakes, like soldiers, police officers, fire fighters, and the person who cleans the restrooms at an elementary school, you start to understand why they like to relax during their time off. It takes someone special to endure risk and the stress that comes with it all the time. But we all face conflict in our lives, and that is what makes them interesting.

That's because conflict can be external or internal. Think of thrillers like the Jack Reacher Series (external) or your favorite romance (internal). The best fiction combines these two things. The brooding detective with internal doubts, the romance where physical distance or circumstances keeps the lovers apart, these are the character-driven conflicts we want to read and write about.

They are what make our characters and their relationships appealing.

The action must take place in an interesting place. The setting does not need to have conflict inherent in it, but it often does. Think of sci-fi and the dangers of space, or Frodo leaving the comfort of the Shire for the dangerous lands beyond it. However, other elements besides conflict can make a setting interesting.

A setting can be beautiful, unusual, historic, or even unique and unfamiliar. Think of *Hunt for Red October* and *30,000 Leagues*

Under the Sea. Both are set in submarines, which for most of us is an unfamiliar location, and therefore interesting.

Lastly, let's look at interesting things being done in an interesting way. Let's think of a story prompt. Ready?

Write me a story about a child setting a table.

Interesting? Could be. Dangerous? Depends on the child. But likely unless you introduce other plot elements (read interesting things) this will be a very short story. Even if the character sets the table in an interesting way, like by tossing the plates and having them land, unbroken, exactly in the places they need to be.

I know someone will pick up this book and go write a story about a child setting a table, and it will be good because it is possible. It is unlikely that they will write an entire novel about this. If you try I would love to read it. Maybe.

Moving beyond our story prompt though, you need to understand plot and pacing. Because not only does it matter where things happen, what things happen, how they happen, and who they happen to or who causes them to happen, it also matters *when* they happen.

Readers of certain genres and books and stories, in general, have come to expect a certain type of plot and a certain pace and timing to events. For them, it is something they notice subconsciously. But as has been shared by writers many times before:

"Nathaniel Hawthorne once said, easy reading is damn hard writing."
-Maya Angelou

That means you, as the author, need to pay attention to the time your story is set in according to reader expectations. A thriller, but set in space or on another planet, is science fiction. A romance set in the Regency period falls into that romance category. And anything set in the past can be historical [insert genre here] but you will have to be sure you get at least the major details of the setting you create right. Readers will know.

So you'll have to do your research. But balance that with not sharing so much of it that your story is no longer interesting. Sound challenging? It can be.

OTHER THINGS YOU NEED TO PAY ATTENTION TO

How do you do that? Well, you don't have to reinvent the wheel, and we have answers. In a later chapter, we will talk about what that looks like.

Next, you need to be able to summarize your work. You need to know your idea so well you can describe it to me in a single paragraph or less. Wait, didn't I just say how complicated this plot thing is? Yep.

But describing your story to someone else should be a simple as saying this one thing:

"My story is about [interesting character] who is caught up [does, finds, goes on a quest for, whatever action they take] for this [interesting thing] in this [interesting way] but has to fight through this [interesting conflict or obstacle] to get there."

You would normally end this with a question. For example, for my novel *Harvested* I would say:

Max Boucher [interesting character] has been hired to find several missing dogs [interesting thing]. But he is battling his own demons and searching for his missing wife [another interesting thing]. Will his investigation [interesting way] lead him to the missing dogs and answers about his missing wife? [interesting conflict].

This isn't super refined and polished. At the time you are plotting it doesn't have to be. You will clean it up when you are in later drafting phases.

All that is left at that point is to set up your writing software so you can be productive as you write. And we will talk about that one last.

There's a resource page on my website where you can find more information about the tools I use and the books I recommend, along with some other free resources.

Some of the links I share will be affiliate links, which means I will get a little commission if you click through and buy something. I will offer advice for using other software throughout this book. For many, I am not an affiliate, but merely directing you either to what works for me or another popular software that I know has brought other writers success.

Remember, I am only sharing what I know about how writers I have talked with create their stories, and the ways I have experienced creati9ng and consuming story. There are other ways of plotting, and within the basic ideas of how people plot, there are an infinite number of variations. They are all equally valid and valuable.

I recommend going through this guide in order first. Then feel free to come back and skip around to areas where you need the most help. Now that you know what the elements of a story are and how we will be proceeding through this book, let's get started on plotting your novel quickly so you can write faster, and hopefully earn more.

DEVELOPING AN INNATE SENSE OF STORY

"What the hell are you talking about, man?"

-The Dude

"I admire your work man! The way you play one side against the other. A true master, a fellow brother shamus!"

-Da Fino

Before we move on to creating your story, I want to talk about one other simple thing: developing an innate sense of story. What does that even mean? As an author you have probably often heard the advice that to be a writer, you must also be a reader. Even Stephen King says so.

Maybe that is what happened with George R.R. Martin. His books were a success, and he stopped reading and moved on to —something else? I don't know what else one would do with their spare time, but then I digress.

The point is that to understand story, you must consume story in some way. You need to read good stories to understand what makes them good. And you need to read bad stories, ones that are simply terrible, at least part way through so you can understand what is wrong with them.

Many authors, myself included, developed this innate sense of story accidentally. I used my library and books as my escape when I was a kid. We weren't rich, so we didn't have cable, and it was pre-computers, so the only windows we had were made of glass, and we ate apples and didn't type on them.

This forced us to do two things: use our imagination when we played outside as children and make up worlds and places we were escaping to. We literally chose our own adventures, sometimes resulting in near serious injury or putting an eye out. We also read, a lot, and as a result we knew a good story from a bad one. We didn't always know what was wrong with a given book, and I could not have defined an inciting incident or a plot point for you at that time, but instinctually, I knew what they were.

Even at age six, I wrote my first "book", a story I created on my own called *George and the Giant Castle*. It wasn't that good, but it did have a beginning, middle, and end, and an adventure in the middle.

But you can further develop this sense of story as an adult and a mature writer, and you can then use it to make your stories better. How? Here are some tips for you:

CONSUME STORIES INTENTIONALLY INSIDE AND OUTSIDE YOUR GENRE

Even as writers, there are times when we watch stories or read books simply for entertainment. Sometimes we need to shut that writing bran off and just love a story for a few moments. But most of the time, we watch or read with the intention of learning something from not only the story, but the creator of the story.

But wait! I said read and watch there, right? Yes. Because when we define consuming a story, in today's world we have lots of choices, from streaming services to audiobooks to short videos. We can consume story in a variety of ways.

I used to recommend reading, and still do, but I broadened my definition of consuming story to the many ways we also tell stories in modern times. So whether you watch, read, or listen, it is really all about story consumption but with intention. For example, I watched the John Wick movies again recently, but I didn't watch them intentionally to study how the story was told, or for the interesting dialog. I watched them to be entertained.

Intentionally watching is what I did with the movie *Nope* and *Everything Everywhere All at Once*. They won awards, and I wanted to see how the creator told the story. What were the plot points? What made it interesting? What tropes and methods did the writers use to make the story better? How can I apply those to my writing?

Two recent examples of genre specific stories I approached intentionally were both *Knives Out* and *Glass Onion*. They are in my genre, and I wanted to answer questions like:

- How did the filmmakers hide the true killer?
- How were clues dropped along the way?
- What red herrings and false clues did they reveal as the story unfolded?
- Did the solution make sense, and could I have figured it out before the ending?

The point was that I watched them not only to be entertained, but to analyze the story as I went. What made it good? What mistakes were made? How could I apply these techniques to my own work, if at all?

I could have gone even a step further and plotted them out in outline form to look even more closely at what the writers did.

CONDUCT IN DEPTH STORY ANALYSIS

One of my favorite television series of all time is *Breaking Bad*. Why? Because Vince Gilligan had an overall plan for the series. Unlike *Law and Order* and all of the variations, this was not a series that would continue ad infinitum. There was a clear outline, a beginning, middle, and end of the series from the start.

Within the seasons of the series, there is also a three-act structure, and if you watch closely, you can see the inciting incident, the midpoint, and the various plot points throughout each season. And to make things even more beautiful, for a plot nerd like me, each episode has a three-act structure as well.

If you study, you can see the dark night of the soul in each season, and the dark night of the soul in the series. The turning points are clear, and the hooks and tropes are ones that anyone writing a cross-genre thriller, whether for television or in novel form, can use to structure your stories.

What does this mean to you (whether you are a Breaking Bad fan or not)? You can take some steps with your own favorite books, films, or television shows:

- Consume with intention, looking for plot points, character development, and more.

- Conduct in-depth story analysis of stories you love.
  Tear them apart and see what makes you love them.
- Analyze stories you do not like. These are stories you
  thought you would like, but quit consuming for some
  reason, not ones you don't like due to genre or personal
  preference. See where the author failed and avoid that
  in your own work.

This helps you hone that sense you likely already have about why a story works and why it doesn't. Then when you are writing and your story goes off the rails, you can "feel" it.

NEVER STOP CONSUMING

Those teachers who tell you to read only the classics are missing some great stuff. First, there have been a lot of great stories written even in the last few years. And on top of that, trends change, and what readers want changes with it. We see this as many of the stories considered classics in the past have not aged well when it comes to language and topics.

Reader attention spans and the way they like to consume stories changes as well. Serial fiction has again become popular (the pulp fiction era and even the shorts shown before movies in theaters long ago are recent modern examples of Raddish and Kindle Vella). As writers, if we want to do this commercially, we must adapt to these trends and respond to them. That does not mean you need to write strictly "to market" but you need to write to a market, and approach readers where they are.

This is a look into the business of writing, and if you don't want to write for a living, but want to write for a hobby, you still want to pay attention to how readers are reading. If you want others to read and love your work, no matter your motive for writing, you never want to be out of touch with the publishing industry and how it currently works.

Not only should you develop an innate sense of story, you need to keep developing it. The longer your write, the better this sense gets, and while your first drafts will never be perfect, they will be better, and continue to improve, if you embrace this technique.

But before we get too far into the weeds, we need to come back to our focus, and talk about where to start when you are plotting, which is, after all, the point of this little guide.

2

DEVELOPING AN INTERESTING CHARACTER OR CAST

"I only mention it because sometimes there's a man... I won't say a hero, 'cause, what's a hero? But sometimes, there's a man. And I'm talkin' about the Dude here. Sometimes, there's a man, well, he's the man for his time and place. He fits right in there. And that's the Dude, in Los Angeles. And even if he's a lazy man - and the Dude was most certainly that. Quite possibly the laziest in Los Angeles County, which would place him high in the runnin' for laziest worldwide. But sometimes there's a man, sometimes, there's a man. Aw. I lost my train of thought here. But... aw, hell. I've done introduced him enough."

-The Stranger

The first thing you need for any story is an interesting character or a group of characters. This can come about in any number of ways. But let's get something out of the way first.

Some writers are more plot-driven than character-driven in their stories. This means the plot is much more important than the character. What happens is generally more important than who it happens to. For example, let's look at James Bond. (RIP Sean Connery, the best Bond. You will be missed.)

Bond is a pretty predictable character who does not experience much growth. He goes after the villain with little care for his own life, defies authority, and always ends up involved with one or more beautiful women in the story. The real interest in the story comes from the plot and what happens. It also comes from the villain, who is arguably the actual hero, or if not the hero, the main character in these stories.

The thing is this: even in a trope-ridden plot-driven story, Bond (and Q, M, and others) are interesting characters. The driver in the story might be the nuclear missile that has been stolen or the assassination plot, or Jaws, a sworn enemy of Bond. The story, however, is still largely dependent on Bond and his crew, and how they interact with one another. Regardless of how static he is over time, Bond is still an interesting character.

One other thing to note, before I get a bunch of hate mail about early Bond and his treatment of women: the character and stories have evolved to adapt to social changes over the years, and the stories are less misogynistic than they used to be. This says more about the growth of the series and the creators than the actual character growth of James Bond himself.

But as we discussed when we talked about developing an innate sense of story, trends change, and the "new" Bond films are more character driven than they used to be, just as the new "doctor" is as well.

But think of the example above: when we are introduced to "The Dude" in *The Big Lebowski* through the monolog of The Stranger, we are quickly shown the truth of these things with the very beginning of the movie. We see that The Dude is indeed lazy, but an interesting kind of lazy, and that the characters around him are equally fascinating, including The Stranger.

One of my favorite character introductions is that of Owen Meany by John Irving: "I am doomed to remember a boy with a wrecked voice—not because of his voice, or because he was the smallest person I ever knew, or even because he was the instrument of my mother's death, but because he is the reason I believe in God; I am a Christian because of Owen Meany."

Through the character, we are also introduced to various aspects of the plot to come. But not everyone starts with character. Sometimes they start with the plot first, and while that can work, it can also create various issues.

THE PROBLEM OF STARTING WITH PLOT

It's not that you can't start with the plot as your idea, but this book assumes that you already have a story idea. The story idea, as we stated above, must have an interesting person in an interesting place doing interesting things in interesting ways. We've defined interesting as something involving conflict, risk, or danger. Maybe even a combination of the above.

In essence, we have a chicken and the egg scenario here. You may have started with a story idea or a character idea, but either way, you need the other elements of story to assist with either one. If you start with character, you still need some interesting things to happen to them, otherwise, you don't have a story, but only a series of events. If you start with a story idea and your plot, you will still need interesting characters to populate it, and that the events of your story happen to and around.

With that in mind, let's break the boring word "interesting" down by how your character is defined.

DEFINING CHARACTER

Your character will be formed in your imagination or that of the reader based on one of two things. A character-driven story will be driven by how the character reacts to any given thing or event. Are they proactive, reactive? Although at the beginning, we know who they are, and at least some of the things that define them, we learn more about them as the story progresses.

In most cases, the reader of more character driven stories is more interested in the who than the what. This is how many cozy mystery writers get away with pretty formulaic mysteries that are not in-depth or difficult to solve. In some cases, they are even pretty predictable. What keeps readers reading? The character of the sleuth, who develops over time, and reacts to things that happen and clues in interesting ways. In short, the character grows, and as they do the reader grows to like or loathe them more.

The other way character is defined is by the type of plot or story. In plot-driven fiction, what happens is more important to the reader than who it happens to. A great example is Dr. Who. The famed series that seems either hated or loved has changed doctors several times. Although every fan seems to have their "favorite doctor" the series goes on. It is the stories that drive the series, not who plays the doctor.

In some genres like epic fantasy, space opera, and other sci-fi, it is a group of characters who are central to the story. These "dream teams" are made up of several individuals, but the group they form often plays the role of the main character. In these cases, the story is almost always more plot-driven than character-driven. Note, however, that the characters who make up the team and the way they interact with each other and the world around them must still be interesting.

The true point is that the genre you write in will often determine the type of story you create (character or plot driven) and will also help define your characters.

CHOOSING THE CHARACTER FOR YOUR STORY AND STYLE

What does all this come down to? You need to develop the character that fits your story, your genre, and your author voice and style. Maybe you will develop a James Bond or Jack Reacher, a character who does not grow or change much even over several books in a series. But Bond and Reacher are both interesting in their own right.

What makes them interesting even though they don't change or grow?

- **Their occupation:** British Spy? Former MP roaming the country and getting into danger? What isn't interesting about that?.
- **Their relationships:** Both men are loners with no deep relationships, but they do seem to have some connections and they make others in each story. These relationships tell us things about them and make them likable.
- **The things they do:** Bond can ski, drive semi-trucks, shoot accurately in odd situations, and fight. Reacher can kick anyone's butt in almost any scenario. He is ultra-sharp and observant, and driven by principle.

I'm sure you can think of more reasons they are interesting characters. Then you can think of other books where the character is what drives the story, and they are so memorable you can hardly get them out of your mind. Immediately the book *A Prayer for Owen Meany* comes to my mind. Owen is a character who, once you have met him, you can never forget.

Which character type is right for your story? Only you can decide, but you must decide. Because even in a plot-driven story, you must have interesting characters.

CHARACTER PROFILES

There are several ways to set up your character profiles. You can choose to use one or more of these methods, but generally, you should have some way you define who your character is, how they look, and important facts about them.

- Describe them. Even if you do not describe them to your reader, describe your characters so you know what they look like. Why so much outcry when Tom Cruise was cast as Reacher for a movie? Because Reacher is described in the books as over six feet tall, and Cruise is —well, not.
- Write a bio and add to it as you go. You will get to know your character more as you write about them, but you need to start somewhere. Start with a simple bio: place of birth, parents' names, where they grew up, accent, sense of style, physical shape, mental deficits, and strengths. As you write and learn more about your character, add those characteristics to your bio.
- Make them take personality tests. You can use anything from Myers-Briggs to Enneagrams. Whatever you like, use it to learn about and flesh out your character.
- Learn about their Cognitive Distortions. It's a little deep in the psychology side, but you can learn a lot about a character through this.

To do these things, you can use tools. Some, like Character Writer (non-affiliate link), will help you reveal character traits and how personality types interact. Others, like the Emotion Thesaurus Series, will help you understand how your character physically responds to various emotional situations.

I use the various templates in Plottr to help me define my characters, and which template I use depends on both the character and the story.

You can also add photos of your characters. You can search for stock images or go to thispersondoesnotexist.com and have an A.I. create one for you. Some people don't like to have images for their characters but prefer to leave them with their imagination and that of the reader. That is also fine, as long as you have a way to picture them in your mind.

I have a friend who is also an artist who sketches her characters. For me, that would not do any good, as they would all look like eggs with faces, but if you are visually talented, it can be beneficial. There is one last general tip I want to share.

A BIT DEEPER ON CHARACTER PERSONALITY

So while we brushed up against character personality in the last section, let's look a little deeper here. Because getting this right can make or break your story. In my case, I like the Enneagram better than some other personality tests, but you can use any of them to add depth to your character.

Essentially you just need to know a few essential things about them, and these things can help shape the story you tell:

- What does your character need? This is not from their perspective, although it can be helpful to think about what they think they need. But in relation to the current story and the conflict they must overcome, what do they need to accomplish their goal? This is usually something internal, although it can also be something physical.

For example, if the theme of your story is justice, your character may need to feel that justice has been satisfied in a given situation, like a murder or some other crime. But the conflict can arise when the definition of justice is not the same as what they thought it was.

Notice that reality and what the character thought conflict. This produces an inner conflict within the theme. But there can be other conflicts that drive the story as well.

- What does your character want? This often conflicts with what they need. When those two things are different, usually in a comedy, the character changes their mind, and decides what they really need is what they want. This comes about through conflicts they experience throughout the story.

For example, your character might want revenge, but what they really need is to see justice done. They will pursue revenge, but at some point along the way, perhaps by seeing the humanity of their adversary, they will decide that justice is greater than vengeance.

How your character does this is largely dependent on their personality type, and if they react in a healthy or unhealthy way. Think of it this way: we all have core fears, what we run away from, and core desires, what we run toward. The question is, "How do you react when your core fear arises?"

If you are a healthy manifestation of your personality type, this reaction will be positive, and if you are in an unhealthy space, it will be negative. Because in fiction we need conflict, most often our characters start out unhealthy and move toward a healthy reaction.

This is called a character arc, or character growth, and you need it to ensure that your readers care about your characters the way you want them to.

Visit that resources page we talked about and you'll find some great books on character arcs and the enneagram. Check them out for an even deeper dive into this topic than we can do here.

But there are other things you can do to make your characters memorable.

GIVE YOUR CHARACTERS A TICK

Maybe not literally. They don't have to have an eye twitch or something but give them something uniquely theirs. This can be a speech pattern or saying, a unique response to some stimuli, a physical reaction or disability, a deformity, or anything else that sets them apart.

This can even be a personality thing, an object they carry, something. If you do this, even for minor characters, it will draw readers deeper into your plot.

Speaking of minor characters, you may have several. They do not all have to have names or be developed at all. Some have a holding place, like GUARD #1 in a movie script or a redshirt in Star Trek. The more characters you have who are developed, the longer your story will probably be.

A good example of a quirk or tick comes from John Irving in *A Prayer for Owen Meany*. Owen is small, lightweight, and has a curiously high-pitched voice described as "ruined." These unique traits all make him a memorable character, but they also all relate to the final resolution of the story. This is a masterful piece of characterization: you too can make your characters memorable, but also make them a vital part of the plot.

Your character types, both major and minor, will also relate to the genre of the story you are writing. Although Shrek is part action-adventure and part romance, most romance stories do not start with a giant green ogre. The type of character will be different for a fantasy or a hard-boiled mystery, although it can be fun to mix genres from time to time.

There are several books on character development, and it is much too deep to cover completely here. Start with these basics though and go from there. Remember, the goal of this book is to provide an overall guide to plotting. Step one is to develop an interesting character or set of characters.

You don't have to develop them perfectly in a single step. Allow yourself to get to know them as your story grows. What's important is to start with a solid foundation, and watch your characters develop both intentionally and organically.

Next, we're going to tackle your setting.

3

CREATING AN INTERESTING PLACE OR SETTING

"Hollywood Star Lanes was a 32-lane bowling alley located on Santa Monica Boulevard in Los Angeles, California. Open from 1960 to 2002, the alley was featured in the film The Big Lebowski, which was filmed on location over three weeks of the eleven-week filming schedule."

-Movie City

What makes a place interesting? Think about it for a moment before you answer and then look around you. Is the place you are right now interesting? If not, what could make it interesting? If so, what's interesting about it?

The bowling alley featured in *The Big Lebowski* was interesting in large part because of how ordinary it was. However, the way the colors and the lanes were filmed, the way the bar appeared, and even the pin setting machines made this place stand out as one of the primary settings in the movie.

If you managed to get there (before it was torn down in 2002) you could easily describe how it looked, how it smelled, and the sounds the balls made striking pins after rolling down the lanes. But it is also interesting because it is the site of conflict, and the only place where we see some of the key characters. It is even featured in the Dude's acid filled dreams.

Your book, like this movie, may have several settings. Some of them are real, or based on reality, and some come more from your imagination and need to be described in more detail. But before we get there, let's talk about setting and conflict, and even about setting as an antagonist.

CONFLICT AND SETTING

Settings can be a place where conflict happens, or it can be a source of conflict itself. A setting can act as a mentor and a helper or even as an antagonist. What do we mean by that?

Let's look at examples. In movies like *The Bourne Identity*, the city where many chases take place is a source of conflict. There are tight turns, narrow streets, and even steps that must be navigated. Obstacles and people must be avoided, and sometimes those obstacles can even cause damage. In this case the setting is not an active antagonist, but it does provide tension and conflict rather than a simple, more neutral setting:

- The setting impedes our protagonist, but only because the antagonist is chasing him.
- The setting also impedes our antagonist from reaching their goal of capturing the protagonist.
- The setting sometimes helps the protagonist by giving him the means to escape his pursuers, or at least put more distance between himself and them.
- The setting is not good or bad, it just is, and must be navigated as a part of the world.

This is true of this setting but think of other movies like *Everest* or *127 Hours*. In both of those cases, the setting is actually the antagonist. Everest kills climbers every single season, and in some ways tries to keep climbers from reaching the summit. While it is not actively doing this, it is a passive antagonist along with the weather and other factors.

In the movie (based on a true story) *127 Hours*, a hiker decides to cut off his own arm to survive, and while there is some debate about whether he had to do that or not, the antagonist was also a part of the setting: the rock his arm was stuck in. There are some who would argue that the rock was not the antagonist, but it was the hiker's own fears.

I say that is not true. The physical thing holding the hiker in place and keeping him from achieving what he needed (to survive) was the rock. He had to make great sacrifices to free himself from the "enemy" to return to the ordinary world, forever changed.

Other examples include *The Martian* and *The Perfect Storm*, both books that later became movies. In both cases, the environment was a direct antagonist to the survival of the main characters.

Setting can be much more than where the action takes place. It can, in many cases, be an integral part of the story, and many would argue that it should be, and almost acts as a character itself.

So when you are creating setting, one of the ways to make a place interesting is to make it a part of the conflict and an influence on the story.

ORDINARY VS. THE EXTRAORDINARY

Settings can be one of two things. It can either be ordinary, exactly what you expect it to be, or it can be extraordinary, something unexpected. For instance, if you say, "Two Irishmen walked into a bar," you may or may not need to describe the bar itself. Most readers have a picture in their minds of what a bar looks like and just a few descriptive terms that reveal what kind of bar this is may be enough to establish your setting, especially if it is not your primary one.

However, if the bar plays a critical role in your story, you may have to go a little deeper. For example, if the bottles behind the bar will be damaged by gunfire or someone will be thrown into them, or they otherwise play a role in the story, you may what to describe the color and type of the bottles. You may even want to mention well-known or expensive brands of liquor to raise the stakes by illustrating their value.

The same is true of anything. A non-descript apartment living room, kitchen, or even a bathroom can be described with minimal need for description. The more description you add to your setting the more importance the reader will lend to that place and that space. Little description = low importance. Detailed description = this place is important and will likely appear more than once in our story.

Think of if we described The Dude's bathroom. It really makes only one appearance in *The Big Lebowski*, but it reveals some key facts about The Dude. The biggest reveal about mistaken identity comes when his assailants accuse him of "his wife owing money all over town."

"My wife?" he says. "Does this place look like I'm married? The toilet seat is up, man!"

Frequently, depending on the genre of a book, world building will demand that you offer more description. If you're describing a planet that is key in your sci-fi epic, you'll need to give the reader an idea of the atmosphere, whether there is water or not, what the pants and inhabitants look like.

In a fantasy, we will need to know about the places where the dragons live, what the villages look like, and what the castles are made of. And even in the case of places you might think of as ordinary, you will need to describe them in detail to your readers.

For example, if your story is set in Seattle, many people who read your book are probably not familiar with the city and some landmarks you might consider common. If something of importance happens in a particular place, you will need to give your readers a sense of that setting.

When describing settings, use all of the tools at your disposal. These are your five senses, and even a sixth, which is the feeling or vibe the place gives off.

- **Sight:** What does it look like? Use this to set the mood you want the reader to feel from the scene. Is it dark, light, dusty, exceptionally clean? All of these can give your reader a sense of what is going to happen in this place, and what it represents.
- **Sound:** Sound tells you a lot about a place. A city street is normally noisy. A bar buzzes with people speaking, perhaps music in the background. These are good descriptions, but it can be even more powerful if the bar is silent or there is no traffic on the streets during rush hour.
- **Smell:** This can be a big one. An unpleasant smell can change the character of your setting. The pleasant scent

of flowers can indicate something good will happen here, or it can be a false clue, an ominous hint that something will go wrong.

- **Touch/Feel:** Not to be mistaken for the vibe mentioned earlier, the feel of carpet between your character's toes, the feel of silk curtains through their hands, or the rough oak of the bar under their fingertips can add a great deal of depth to your scenes. Remember, describe only what your reader needs to know to understand the setting and how important it is.
- **Taste:** While this can be tricky with setting, the air can have a taste to it. So can water, or another beverage, or food in a restaurant. Use this sense carefully—overdone it can seem cliché and even out of place. But when used well, your scene will come to life in an entirely different way.

Remember to use the unusual. we expect that for the most part hospitals will be clean and well kept. They may be crowded, and that in itself may tell us something about our story. But if a hospital is unkept, run-down, and dirty your reader will want to know details about its condition. How did it become run down? Is there peeling paint, broken windows, and dingy walls? Is the floor dirty? The windows? The walls? Is the outside different from the inside?

Setting can actually become a character in your story, a vital part of your tale.

Besides expected and unexpected and the detail of description you should offer, there are two categories of setting to be aware of.

THE WORLD AROUND US

The world around us lets us know what kind of story this is and how the world operates. For example, if the world where the run-down hospital is located is a post-apocalyptic one where everything is run down, it can help define the world around it by letting the reader know just how bad things are.

If the world around the hospital is a normal, modern one, the presence of the run-down hospital itself presents a conflict with reality, and that can often bring the setting into the story in a way that furthers the plot and raises tension.

But the world around us also tells us about genre. A stone castle or a fort made of wood can tell us the time the story is set in. The presence of a moat and dragons can tell us we are reading a fantasy, and a ship floating in space tells us we are reading a science fiction story.

Think of your world setting as the canvas on which you are painting your story. It is where your characters will live and move. The bigger the canvas, the more epic and larger the story is. For instance, the Milky Way would be a poor setting for a short story as we would have little time to explore all of it. Contrariwise, it is difficult to write a novel that occurs all in one room, although it has been done.

Like the cast of characters, the setting can help you define the breadth and type of your story.

A WORD BEYOND PLOT

There are things that happen in the English language that you don't think much about unless you become a writer or study linguistics. But adjectives happen in a certain order in sentences. You say "the big blue house" not "the blue big house."

In the same way, the order sense appear in your fiction makes a difference as well. It's a psychological trick that engages readers without them even knowing it.

The order you present the senses in matters. This is called KAV:

- **Kinetic.** If you appeal strongly enough to your character's sense of motion, like crawling, walking, running, fidgeting, or other senses related to movement.
- **Audio.** The next sense to engage is sound. As your character moves into or through your setting, what do they hear? What does the setting sound like?
- **Visual.** Finally, describe what the character sees. This engages the reader in the same way they notice things when they enter a new place or scene. You can repeat this cycle over and over.

Remember, KAV your settings. Then add other senses for additional depth to your description. But following this order will hook your reader in a unique way. This is more about writing, than plotting, but you can make these three things central to the descriptions you give your readers, the places you describe will come to life.

SMALLER SETTINGS INSIDE LARGER ONES

Within your larger world, you will have smaller settings as well. These don't have to be fully developed in your outline, but it may be helpful to at least have a general idea of what they might be. For example, each of my *Capital City Murders* novellas has several settings:

- The State Capitol Building

- The city where the capitol building is located, referred to generally (Denver, Boise, Salt Lake City, for example)
- The hotel where Nick, our protagonist is staying
- Restaurants he visits
- The crime scene
- A police station, newspaper office, and other locations.

For this series, generally the most important of these are the capitol building and the crime scene, but other settings can be important as well. The key is that before writing each one, I know something about each setting and what will happen there.

If you think about your favorite book or movie, you can think of the world as a whole (The Game of Thrones kingdoms) and more micro-settings, like the North Wall. This is universal to every story.

Whether your setting is a farm or a library or a forest, it is contained in a larger world defined by when and where your book is set.

HOW MUCH TIME SHOULD I DEVOTE TO SETTING

This book is an overall guide to plotting, and you may think that all of these things I have talked about so far seem time-consuming. They don't have to be. Let's break it down to something simpler. Let's say I am writing a fantasy. I can define my setting like this:

- The World: A place where dragons, elves, dwarves, and fairies exist, and magic plays a role in everyday life.
- A castle within that world: large, stone, cold, surrounded by a moat and protected by soldiers stationed along the wall and in various parapets.

- The enchanted forest: where many of the creatures live and a dangerous place for humans who have not been invited.
- The swamp: a place where dark, dangerous creatures live. No one has crossed it successfully.

The details can come as I write, or I can fill them in before I start, but just knowing the basic facts is enough to set up the plot. The fact is, I will probably add settings like rooms in the castle and tunnels underneath as the story is developed. But with a framework to start with, adding those becomes easy.

And not every single place needs a detailed description before I start writing my draft. From the short description of the castle above, I can imagine and describe what the tunnels underneath might look like.

There have been dozens of books written about developing settings. I recommend *A Writer's Guide to Active Setting* to get you started.

You can research and read a variety of them, peruse and even attend classes at conferences that talk about setting, but if you are looking to simply set up the plot for your story, the basics are enough for you to get started.

Next, we will start to talk about what happens to your **characters** in your **setting**, and what interesting things they will do.

DOING INTERESTING THINGS

"The ringer, Dude. The whites! We throw out the ringer, I grab one of them, and beat it outta them. It's gonna be great!"

-Walter

You can start with a great character in a great setting, but things will get dull quickly if they just sit down with a glass of wine to read *War and Peace*. Even if they are reading a more interesting piece of literature or shopping for new slacks or enjoying a cup of coffee, pretty soon something interesting has to happen that disrupts their ordinary lives.

That's why almost every single type of story structure starts with one thing first: the reader is introduced to the world as it is normally. So your character could be enjoying some avocado toast and a light roast half-caff blonde espresso with extra whip at their favorite coffee shop if that is normal for them. That can certainly be your opening scene. But something needs to disrupt that normal fairly quickly.

Setting this scene can take some time for certain genres, and it is best if you can show us this world rather than just telling us about it. For example, if you write epic space opera sci-fi, we are going to need to picture ships, planets, and the vastness of space. This can be done quickly, but the world must deepen at some point, and bouncing through hyperspace at light speed is not normal for most of us, even though Elon Musk is dreaming about it right now.

The same can be said for epic fantasy. We need to understand the creatures who live in this place and time, the magic system and how it works, and the unusual plant life, animals, and other things that result from the world being as it is. Setting the scene can be as simple as a coffee shop for some books, or a chapter or even two in an epic fantasy.

A great example of this is Hunger Games. In this case, we learn a lot about the world around us through what Katniss does and what happens to her. We see her hunting for food, trading her kill in a market, and we see the poverty of the world she lives in. We hear about The Reaping, an event in which children were chosen to participate in the mandatory Hunger Games.

In this way we learn, through being shown, not told, many facts about this world, the politics of it, and at least one way the government controls the people. There is no long exposition, but rather a revealing series of events.

The point is at the start, you are going to have to grab your reader by something interesting happening. In a murder mystery, a man with a gun could burst into the coffee shop and kill someone, or the avocado toast could be poisoned and the character you introduced could die (I like that one, to be honest, or some other violent act or death could kick off the plot.

For a romance, the love interest could walk in, taking the breath away from the caffeine averse heroine. Or you could have a "meet-cute" where one spills their drink on the other or asks about the book they are reading, or he trips over the woman's shoes, sprawling into the fireplace and breaking his nose. Okay, that's a "meet ugly" but hey, did you think I would get through a scenario without adding violence and blood?

Back to our plot. Essentially this disruption of normal life is how we start our plot. This is the hook.

Note that this does not have to be an "inciting incident" which we will talk more about in a moment. It just introduces the reader to the fact that "things were normal, and now they are not as normal."

Keep in mind that the normal world is often not that boring. For a detective, the ordinary wold can show them in a car chase or an making an arrest. For them, this is normal. A knight can be in a fight, a spaceship captain can be engaged in battle, and our romantic heroine could be a skydiving thrill seeker.

You will want to learn more about hooks, what they are, and why they work. I recommend *Hooked*, by Les Edgerton. It's a great place to start, and we'll talk about them briefly again later.

Once we have hooked the reader, it's time to look at some other elements of "doing interesting things."

THE INCITING INCIDENT

The guy walking into the coffee shop and our couple meeting is not the inciting incident necessarily. The inciting incident is what draws our character and therefore the reader into the main part of the story. "And what is the main part of the story?" you ask.

The primary conflict. Conflict is central to plot. If we don't have it, we don't have much of a story. To know what the conflict is, we need to know several things about our character and the story itself, some of which we have talked about when it comes to character development and settings.

But before we go further, we need to talk about what, exactly, an inciting incident is, and why it is different from a hook. A hook lets us know something interesting is going to happen. The man walking in the coffee shop with ominous music in the background is a hook. Even when the shooting starts, that might still be a hook.

The inciting incident is what kicks off the character's journey. At this point the hook has led to us knowing the theme of your story. It has often even been stated by the main character or someone has stated it for them or directly to them.

For example, in the example of *The Hunger Games*, the theme seems to be survival. But the theme is actually much deeper than that. It's about writing an epic wrong, and "winning" will involve beating the capitol at their own game.

This sets up the conflict between what Katniss wants and what she actually needs, between her external goal, to win the Hunger Games and survive, and her internal goal, which is living up to her true potential in many areas of her life. This becomes the theme of the entire series.

The inciting incident is when she volunteers to take the place of her younger sister Prim. At that point, her feet are set on the journey to the new world, and there is no turning back. This is also sometimes called the Catalyst.

The conflict set up by your character's goals combined with the inciting incident is what gets your story rolling. To look at this in greater depth, we're going to look at Goals, Motivations, and ultimately the conflicts that result.

YOUR CHARACTER'S GOAL

To do interesting things, your character needs to have an interesting goal. But what makes a goal interesting? The truth is, anything you want it to be.

You can make almost any goal interesting, from winning a boxing match (*Rocky*) to escaping a prison (*The Shawshank Redemption*) to traveling to see a dead body (*Stand by Me*). Also, keep in mind that the visible, physical goal is not always the internal, personal goal of the hero. There are often hidden goals, hidden motives, and ones we discover as we write our stories.

The inciting incident is the moment when the protagonist, your hero, is knocked off their current path in the ordinary world toward those goals. Even though the character may not be aware of their internal goals or their actual needs, usually your story starts with the main character wanting something.

In the movie The Big Lebowski, the external goal is simple to define. "All the dude ever wanted was his rug back, man." It's simple, but interesting, and it sets off a series of events that lead The Dude through various moments of self-realization, and even moments of being "very un-Dude."

What makes these goals even more interesting? Motive.

THE VALUE OF MOTIVE

The second thing we need to talk about is motive. Because for your character to do interesting things, they need to have a motive to do so. A motive is simply the reason your character will act in the way they do, or their "why."

In the movie *Taken* (and *Taken 2*, *Taken 3*, and the lesser-known *Taken Aback*) the father's motive is to recover his daughter, someone who has been taken from him, and to exact revenge on the kidnappers. The goal is so strong and noble, nothing will stand in his way.

Every character in every book or every movie you can think of, even the bad ones, has a goal of some sort and they have a clear and compelling reason to move toward that goal.

The motive must be realistic and powerful enough to move the character through hardships. They can think about giving up when things are hard, but their motive must be enough for them to keep trying. Unless you are writing noir, in which case your character can give up and die when your story ends, but that is a niche market for—well, I'm not sure who even reads that. If it's you, I'm sorry. Feel better. Eat a cookie. Or Ice cream. That works too.

Would the motive be enough to get someone to do extraordinary things? A kidnapping of a daughter or loved one is powerful. The desire for a jelly donut, while it can be powerful, is not enough to carry most people through significant hardship and conflict (which your novel has, right?).

Everyone in your story needs a motive. Why did the kidnappers take the daughter in the first place? Money? Fame? Just to irritate daddy? Be sure their motive is great enough to entice them to perform an illegal act that comes with significant risk of punishment.

Heist books and movies are a great example of this. All that money in that bank vault is a good motive, or those bonds and securities, or whatever thing of value the thieves are trying to steal. Motives can be murky to the reader at first, but you must know as a writer what they are pretty clearly. This is the only way you can hide them from the reader and slowly reveal them over time.

But think of movies like *Gone in Sixty Seconds*, with Nicholas Cage. The motive, on the surface, appears to be to steal a bunch of cars to satisfy a list that will get his brother out of trouble and save his life. However, the true motive is revealed as we go along: Cage must beat his nemesis by stealing a Mustang called Elenore, and to "win" by beating his antagonist, and detective determined to catch him and his ring of car thieves.

This becomes the primary motive for a portion of the story, overwhelming even his external motive to save his brother's life. It becomes about the internal goal represented by a single car, and one that is of vital importance to his identity and his future.

Secondary characters also need motive. If the police help the private detective while feeding him clues, why would they do that? What is their motive? If they don't have one, it is hard for the reader to believe that the police chief would call the novelist or the photographer at all, or let them see confidential police files, or bring them into the investigation. Secondary character's motives are just as important as those of your main characters.

Also vital to your story is the motive of your antagonist. Usually their goals are either the opposite of your protagonist, or the same. In the case of opposites, your antagonist wants an entirely different outcome than your protagonist. They work against each other, like the thief who wants to steal a large sum of money, and the cop who wants to protect it. Note that the motives are as different as the goal.

If they are the same, the two can be in a race toward the same goal, but usually their motives are opposing. Both can be looking for a lost object or artifact, one of them to keep it out to the hands of the bad guys, the other to use the power that comes with it for evil.

This is why both the story arc and the character arc of your protagonist and antagonist often move in opposite directions: motive. This is a great source of tension and conflict, which are the essential ingredients to your story.

It is not enough for someone to be motivated though. They must also have something else: the means to achieve their goals.

You often hear this when it comes to mysteries, but it is true of other genres as well, and helps us lead to the final piece of our goal, motivation, and conflict puzzle: conflict. So before we get there, let's take a small detour into means, or your character's abilities.

YOUR CHARACTER'S ABILITIES

A housewife is attacked and suddenly kicks the asses of several well-trained military guys who broke into her house. Really? Where did she get her training? How did she overpower them all? Why didn't one of them just shoot her? Why did they come at her one at a time instead of in a group? So many questions.

For this to happen, you have to suspend the disbelief of your reader or viewer. I won't believe a housewife has those abilities unless you convince me she got them somewhere, and she also has a certain level of super-human strength and endurance.

If you haven't ever checked it out, you should look at the YouTube channel called Honest Action where a couple of guys go through movies and talk about how quickly the hero would be dead, how many times they would have died or been critically injured, and how unrealistic they are. Why do we keep watching?

Because the writers and producers can convince us that the hero can do things that are not humanly possible, even if they are human. Take any Arnold Swartzenagger movie, the Die Hard movies, most kung fu or martial arts movies, and pretty much any films with a fight scene outside a ring. We believe because we have been shown (not told) how strong a character is.

We also don't read books or watch action movies for everything to be realistic. The key is to make the reader believe how tough your main character is and lead them to the understanding that they can do almost anything. To do this, you combine both motive (powerful, realistic motive) with means.

John Wick is a martial arts expert and great with a gun and an extremely strong motive. No, his fight scenes are not realistic, but we believe he is such an expert he can do the impossible. Therefore we still watch.

How, exactly do you do this? By showing us an ordinary world where your character does extraordinary things as a part of their daily routines. You can show us the housewife has extraordinary reaction skills when her child knocks a vase off a table, and she catches it effortlessly. Or you hero can chase someone down who seems like they should be faster than them.

The important thing is to early, and often, suspend our disbelief through first showing us the simple things your character can do, and sometimes showing their weaknesses as well. The more normal their abilities appear, the less likely we are to disbelieve them when they do something more complex.

The other important thing is that you follow your own rules. If you have set up a magic system, your characters must operate inside those lines. If you show that your character has certain strengths and weaknesses, you have to remain consistent with what they can and cannot do.

Readers need to know the characters in your stories from their personalities to their abilities, because that is how you make the conflict in your story believable. But first, a word about opportunity.

OPPORTUNITY KNOCKS

Your character also needs one more thing to make the things they do both interesting and believable: opportunity. In mysteries, this is often the trifecta and what convicts someone of a crime:

- Motive
- Means
- Opportunity

For the detective to catch them, he must prove that they have all three. So while your character can have a goal, if they don't have the motive, means, and opportunity to achieve that goal, it simply isn't possible. Readers will have a hard time believing they did it.

What does opportunity mean to characters beyond the mystery genre? Well, if the female lead in a romance meets her dream man in France near the Eiffel tower, she must either live in France or she must have traveled there somehow, which means she had an opportunity.

That could be a vacation, a trip with a friend, or a year of study abroad. If the same character decides to stay in Paris for longer to explore this new romance, they must have some opportunity to do so: extended vacation, additional funds for a place to stay, etc. This also applies to each action they take in your story.

If your character is going to go on a long journey in space, they need a ship, a suit, and probably someone to finance the trip, even if they have the means themselves. They must have the time to take the trip and the motive which causes them to leave their normal life and act on that opportunity.

You can see how quickly these things all intertwine. For your character to do interesting things, they need to have an interesting goal—something readers relate to. They also need to have an interesting motive which leads them to pursue that goal. Obstacles need to be placed in the way of that goal, and their motive must be strong enough to inspire them to face and overcome those obstacles.

But they also must have the means to do so. People do not wake up good sword fighters, dragon slayers (or trainers, your preference), or great photographers or writers. They must learn, practice, and hone their skills to get the means to fight (or write) effectively.

Finally, they must have opportunity. There must be a way for them to become involved in the quest, mystery, romance, or space adventure. If you have all of those ingredients for your story, your character will never lack interesting things to do.

Finally, your all of these things will combine to produce conflict. This can be from conflicting goals or motives, needs or wants, and even the abilities they have or don't have. Strengths, weaknesses, opportunity or lack of it, can all work together and produce conflict. And conflict introduces interesting ways the events that are in your story happen.

Let's move on to the interesting ways they will do things, but only briefly, because we want to move right into the meat of plot and pacing and truly developing your story.

38

5

THINGS HAPPEN IN AN INTERESTING WAY

"I'm just sitting here, finishing my coffee."

-Walter

As with the other aspects of your plot, there are a lot of things you can do to make the way things happen in your story interesting. Have you ever read a book where you got to the point where the character was just—driving? Walking? Getting from one place to the other? They may not have even been thinking and mulling over the events around them, but pretty soon, things would just be—boring.

If a dragon darted out, and their car crashed into it, that would be interesting. If their mode of transportation is interesting (like a camel - watch out, they spit!) that could be interesting, for a while.

There's more to this than your character getting from place to place though. Your character must also have things that set them apart from other characters, otherwise, you'll just have a bunch of cardboard cutouts moving around in your story. The things they do must be done in an interesting way.

If you are tired of the word "interesting" you can substitute something else, but the key is that your story, no matter what shape it takes, must never, ever, ever bore the reader. A good writer friend of mine Michaelbrent Collings (horror and multi-genre author, look him up) has several rules of writing, and one of the simplest is this: "you bore me, you lose me."

This includes the way your characters do nearly everything they do, like talk, walk, get from place to place, live, eat, drink, fight, love (looking at you *Fifty Shades of Ick*), and anything else they do. Let's take a quick closer look at those things.

DYNAMIC DIALOGUE

I will never tire of saying this, but even if you don't use a single dialog tag other than an occasional "he said" or "she said" (unless you have three or four minor characters in the room) each character should have their own voice, and I should be able as a reader to tell who is speaking almost from the first word they say.

Each should have their own unique set of words they use, the order they use those words, and the way they pronounce them or use them in specific context, just like people do. Even if your best friend does not have a distinctive, booming voice, you can often identify them speaking on the phone or even in a crowded room because you know *how* they talk. The reader wants to know your character that well, which means you need to know them that well first.

A note on dialect: one way to set a character apart is by using dialect, but too much dialect is exceptionally hard to read. Like I will stop reading your book and throw it across the room hard to read.

Dialect is like salt—a little gives us a taste for your characters and who they are. Too much, and we gag a bit. If a character drops their "g's" on "ing" words, for example, you don't need to drop every single one. Just drop the first few, and our minds will understand "this character drops their g's" without your need to do it every time. It doesn't hurt to remind the reader from time to time. It is the same with a southern, British, or Australian accent. A little goes a long way. .

Think of these two sentences:

"We can sit and talk it over. Would you like a cup of tea?"

"Sure, we can chat? How about a spot of tea and a biscuit?"

There's no heavy dialect or accent, but my bet is that you can tell the difference between two characters pretty quickly because of the words they use and the order they are in. You can probably think of some famous lines from movies or often quoted ones that you recognize right away. You know who said them because of the way they said them.

Dialog reveals a lot about your character, including their education level, where they are from, and what they think of themselves (and therefore what the reader thinks of them). During the plotting process, think about who your characters are and how to make the way they talk unique and interesting. This will shape how you write your draft, and how much revision you need to do later.

Another important point is authors often don't pay enough attention to. Be careful about using accents to define people of race, color, ethnic origin, etc. It is really easy to offend someone. I recommend having "sensitivity' readers that you send your prose to if you are going to write a POC character and you are not a member of that ethnic group yourself. Things that seem innocent to you may not be perceived that way, and that can really hurt your book sales and even your career.

The more you listen to people talk, the better you will become at writing dialogue. And if you don't listen to your books out loud already as you edit them, at the very least either read your dialogue out loud or have your computer or someone else read it to you. You will quickly "hear" the flaws and can correct them.

TRANSPORTATION AND WALKING

If you are writing sci-fi or fantasy, one of the things that can make your story more interesting is how people get from place to place. For instance, if everyone walks everywhere, footwear might be a very important part of your plot.

But you can make transportation and how someone or everyone gets from place to place an important and therefore interesting side of the story. From a nice old car to a special form of wagon to riding on the back of a dragon named Toothless, transportation is one way to make the way things happen in your story interesting.

Transportation can be a great world-building technique. You can let the reader know early in your world building what kind of world you have created simply by showing them how people get from place to place. This helps you build your interesting setting, and how your character reacts to this form of transportation also helps you build interesting characters.

The way your character travels can reveal details about their lives. The Lincoln Lawyer, who does a lot of his business from the back of his Lincoln (with a driver) rather than in his office is a quirk that reveals who he is and helps us relate to him. In my

Max Boucher series, Max drives a 1969 Buick Skylark, not a typical old muscle car, but in my opinion one of the coolest. What makes that more interesting is why he drives that car, and refuses to use something else as his daily driver.

In several of the stories about him, his car is a vital part of the plot.

Considering transportation can be a part of world building, character development, and your characters doing things in interesting ways.

WAY OF LIFE

Think of how the Hobbits lived in the shire, and how that changed when they embarked on a great journey. In my book, *Harvested*, my detective lives in an apartment over a bar in Seattle even though he owns a home in Queen Anne, a relatively wealthy district. There is a distinct reason (read motive) for this and it adds a layer of interestingness (it's a word, I promise) to his way of life.

No matter what genre you are writing, your characters have a way of life. They are either rich or poor, and they feel different ways about their current status. Think of Ready Player One, Mad Max, and even John Wick. Another great example is Jack Reacher, a rouge agent who is essentially homeless, wandering from place to place because he knows if he settles down, his life as he knows it will be over.

This defines the way he does things and makes them even more interesting than they might be otherwise.

The way your characters live will help them behave in interesting ways that intrigue the reader and help them identify with them.

DINNER AND COCKTAILS

Food and drink are also interesting ways to flesh out your story, so to speak. The key when you are building your world in your mind is that you write these things down. Make them a part of your plot, and make sure you understand the "rules" of your world and your characters.

Your character could love black licorice (yuck) and always have some with him. Or he could chew gum, suck on mints, or just have odd eating habits. Maybe he is an alcoholic or a recovering one. Maybe the food and drink of your world help set it apart from others.

There is also the issue of food security. If food is scarce, this can affect how your characters operate and live daily. Think of the start of Aladdin and his thefts from the market. That glimpse tells us a lot about the society he lives in and his own situation.

And think of how your character eats. They can consume food in an interesting way, and this can even be one of their "quirks." This can be especially powerful if this ends up being critical to the plot or the resolution of your story.

KUNG FU FIGHTING

Surely not everyone was Kung Fu fighting? Well, that is true. Everyone is probably not Kung Fu fighting, and not everyone is good at it, but you can reveal a lot about your world by how the people in it fight.

- What weapons do they use?
- What style do they fight in? One adapted from the real world, or one you have made up?
- Is their society a violent one or a peaceful one?

- Is there an ongoing war, threat of war, or coming invasion?

All these things not only affect your plot and conflict, but they reveal how your characters live. During the threat of war, people can be on edge and stressed, and it times of peace in a peaceful society, even a small threat of war or an unusual individual bent on violence can be disruptive and cause conflict.

HOW THEY LOVE

Historical romances and fantasy romances often include arranged marriages and unrequited love. Think of *Shrek* or *The Princess Bride*. Action? Adventure? You bet, but primarily driven by love and the conflict it produces.

How your characters and those in your world love lets them do things in an interesting way. This love also helps drive your plot, because inevitably fictional love (and even real-life love, if we are honest) breeds conflict.

This is a good place to mention that different kinds of love are not only okay but encouraged in your fiction. LGBTQ+ characters are largely underrepresented in fiction, although that is changing. But do not include these characters just to be politically correct or such nonsense. Write authentic characters, and if you are not a member of these communities, have sensitivity readers or friends in the community who can read your stories and let you know if you got things wrong.

Also, understand that the way your characters love and how detailed your descriptions of that love are with both make some readers happy and also make some of them angry. Understand your genre and your audience. For example, you can certainly have a romance subplot in a mystery, but if it begins to take over the story, some readers will not be happy. After all, they bought a mystery, not a romance.

The same is true for the heat level of your stories. Military sci-fi readers may not want to read a steamy sex scene after the battle in the same way someone who purchased a clean romance won't tolerate scenes that are "too hot." But if you are writing a steamy romance? You better bring the heat, or your readers will feel cheated.

Love is important no matter what genre you write, so be sure to consider it as you plan your stories.

IN CONCLUSION

The key is that you don't have to include all of these things in your plot. Do you need to have them all figured out before you move on to the next chapter and plot and pacing? No. But if you have a list and at least an idea about some of them, it will help you tell better stories.

So far we have characters in interesting places who have some interesting things to do in an interesting way. That's a start, but now we are going to pull all those ideas together.

If you are a discovery writer and you have made it this far, good for you. We are about to start the actual plot or outline of our book. This might scare you a little, but you don't need to be frightened. You can go to the first part of the next chapter and skip the rest if you want, or you can follow us a little farther and find out why plotters do the things we do.

You certainly don't have to. Stephen King claims to hate outlines, but he always has an idea of how the story will end, and usually about some events that will happen along the way. I would argue that is at least a skeleton of an outline.

I would also argue that his editors could be a little more heavy-handed. But he has such a unique sense of story built into his brain, he can get away with a loose outline with no problem at all.

Most of us can't do that, and the result is that we need either a more robust outline or several drafts to get there. But the faster we write, and the fewer drafts we have to create, the more time we will have to write more books. And no matter what your writing goals, that's a good thing. But we'll talk about that at the very end of the book.

So let's get into the meat of this thing: plot and pacing. Stick with me. I promise this chapter will make it worth all the work you have put in so far.

6

PLOT AND PACING

"New information has come to light."

-The Dude

So we started with the premise that your story must have interesting characters in an interesting place doing interesting things in an interesting way. Most of what we have said so far has been built on that premise. That's not enough, though. For your story to work, you need to tell it in a certain order. Because a story must also have three basic parts.

At a minimum, your story needs to have a beginning, middle, and end. This is the simplest form of plotting, and if you are a discovery writer, I highly recommend the book *Take Off Your Pants*. Note that I said the book, not to take off your pants (provided you were wearing any in the first place). I don't need to know, and I certainly don't need those images in my head. Moving on.

The book provides a simple outline and the template is also available in Plottr (the #1 visual outlining software for writers).

For those who are discovery writers or just dipping their toes in the plotting waters, it provides a great place to start.

Before you run off, buy that book, and ignore the rest of this one though, let's look at the three parts of the story from a high level, and then we will go a little deeper. For you discovery writers, hang in there just a little longer.

THE BEGINNING

There are two parts to the beginning, or two beginnings to be exact. There is the hook—the thing that gets the reader reading the story in the first place. You should have hooks throughout your story as well: earlier I mentioned the book Hooked by Les Edgerton and it's a great place to start learning about them.

Again, don't run off. We'll talk about hooks when we dive deep, but you have your first hook, the really exciting thing that makes the reader sit up and say, "Show me more." That hook (and a few more) is how you get your audience from the start to the inciting incident, which is where the conflict actually begins.

- The first part of your book is to do just a few simple things:
- Introduce the reader to your characters and the world as it is.
- Introduce tension and the stakes for the main character and perhaps the antagonist.
- Get the reader to the inciting incident and the beginning of the conflict.

That's it. There are tons of books out there that talk about great beginnings, how vital opening lines and opening scenes are, and more. You should check them out and use the ones that work for you. The point is really that no matter how you do it, the beginning of your book must grab reader attention and keep it until you introduce the true stakes and conflict in your story.

For your initial plot, all you need to have mapped out is the first hook and the inciting incident, and you as the author should have a good idea of what events will lead from one of those events to the other.

This can be as simple as one notecard or post-it note, or a scene card in Plottr. Or if you are a thorough plotter, it can be several events and scenes. This also depends on your type of story. In a mystery, this will be a rapid transition, and the inciting incident (the crime) will often happen early. In epic fantasy, the inciting incident could be pushed back further to allow for world building and development, but even then, there should be several hooks in the beginning to pull the reader along until we reach that point.

Remember showing, not telling is the way to keep your reader engaged. Don't describe a kitchen, show someone cooking, and don't describe the food. Show someone eating, and describe it using all five senses: taste, smell, feel, sound (crunch?), and what it looks like.

Early on, we need to see what our main character has-what is normal -- so we can also see what they have to lose. In nearly every case, the primary protagonist must be introduced before or at the inciting incident. Also, a note on the inciting incident is not always what you think it would be.

For example, in a mystery, it is not always when the crime occurs. It is when the detective is set on the journey to solve it. In a fantasy, it may not be when the village is wiped out by the dragon, but it is when the hero decides to go search for the dragon to kill it. The inciting incident is when the journey, story, or main conflict starts.

As you move past the inciting incident, this is where the middle of your book begins.

THE HOPEFULLY-NOT SAGGING MIDDLE

The middle of the story is often where writers struggle, and like many of these other topics, there are entire books that talk about avoiding the sagging middle and what to do to make your book compelling all the way through.

Why does the middle sag from time to time? First, it is not necessarily the middle of the story that sags, but part of the middle. See, we have to get our character from that inciting incident to the mid-point of the book and then to the final fight and climax. The problem with journeys is they can be—well, boring. The route across Nevada, Nebraska, or even parts of New Mexico is example enough if you have ever driven them.

How do you avoid the sagging middle? A few simple points in your outline could help.

- A Try/Fail or Two: This is where the antagonist thinks they have the answer to their problem, but they really don't, and they fail to solve it. Usually, they learn something from this failure.
- A Missed Opportunity: These can work well with romance and some other genres as well. Essentially there is a path to the answer that is time sensitive, and your main character misses it.
- A Change in Location: Change the location where things are happening to change things up.

- A Strong Sub-Plot: If you have a strong B-plot that ties back into your main plot in the resolution, this can help your story to avoid sagging.

Perhaps the most important thing to remember is that both tension and conflict should increase, never decrease. Things should get harder for your character as your book moves forward, not easier.

However, there are a few common errors writers make. The first is that your protagonist finds things too easy. Obstacles are much too simple to overcome, and so he or she has much too easy a time of it. Think of if there was a Superman movie without Kryptonite or his true weakness, Lois Lane (don't get me started. I mean it.)

The second error, though, is if your character simply cannot catch a break. No matter what they do there are not even small victories. In this case, the plot stagnates because although things should get harder, they should never be truly impossible. They can seem difficult and near impossible, but anything that requires some kind of miracle to overcome dances into a dangerous area.

Your character also must learn from failure. Each Try/Fail even if the results are horrible, must teach your character something. They need to come out of the ordeal with a new piece of information, another clue, or perhaps a new tool they can use to eventually solve the primary conflict in the story.

Another error? The conflicts happen in the wrong order. Each try/fail should escalate and get harder until the midpoint (the major turning point in the story) and then the dark night of the soul. If we have a really difficult problem followed by one that is much simpler to solve, it breaks the rising action cycle readers love, and gets, well, boring.

Of course, we are just scratching the surface here. There are tons of blog posts, books, and workshops on this topic. A quick Google search will reveal a plethora of them, and nearly every plot template out there tries to address the sagging middle in one way or another.

The key is that even with a loose outline you should at least have a vague idea of the kind of trials your character will face, or what "rocks" you will be throwing at them. Knowing this will keep your story moving, keep the middle from sagging, and get you well on the way to writing the end. And finishing that first draft is the ultimate goal.

THE ENDING OR RESOLUTION OF YOUR STORY

Stick with me discovery writer guy, because your hero, Stephen King, even has something to say on this. Arguably the greatest "anti-outline" guy in the history of the world says that even without an outline, he has a good idea where the story is going before he starts.

Now, he might start with a much broader destination than some of us would prefer, but he at least has an idea. For example, if you are writing a romance, you might simply have the idea that the hero and the heroine find each other again in the enchanted forest and escape to the castle of love where they live happily ever after. Is that enough?

Well, that depends on you and how much direction you need. If the ending is too vague, you may get lost along the way. If it is too specific, many writers will freeze, finding that crafting the journey to get precisely there is much too restrictive for their muse.

To determine what you need as a writer, you might have to play with things a little bit to get them right. My advice is to start with simple methods of plotting and refine them as you go. Have a general idea of your ending, and you can refine that as you write and get to know your characters and stories better.

The key to the ending is that it must be satisfying to the reader, which means all of those subplots and stories you have created along the way need to be wrapped up neatly. This means for a mystery, all those clues need to be resolved, either as false ones or as a part of the solution. You can't leave that fantasy side quest out there hanging. Your reader wants to know how things turned out.

The ending is also related to your genre. Romance must end Happily Ever After or Happily for Now. Mysteries must resolve the main crime in this story, even if there is a subplot that continues throughout the series. Fantasy must end one quest even if it hints at another. The same is true for any other genre.

How you get there may differ, and what that ending looks like will certainly vary, but the common thread is that the reader must be satisfied, at least if you want them to keep reading your work long term.

These three elements are the essentials of plot. What is this pacing thing I am talking about?

THE BEAT GOES ON

As you research story structure, you will start to understand something that rose out of plays, film and to an extent music that we use in writing. It has, of course, always been a part of story, but it is perhaps better defined now than it ever has been.

I'm not going to try to explain this exactly in music terms, because although I love music, playing it is not one of the talents I have, and any attempt to walk down that trail with this information is a sure way for me to spill the tune I would be trying to carry in the proverbial bucket.

I'm just going to say that if you listen to any well-constructed song, especially one that has gone viral other than for the reason that its lyrics contain the initials WAP, which I thought stood for "Wicked Apple Pie" until an embarrassing moment attending something that turned out to be more than a dessert sharing party. But I digress.

Even "Gangnam Style" or the further back Ramstein tune, "Du Hast" were both exceptionally popular and repeatable even though most people listening to them had no idea what the lyrics meant. That is because the beats of the music and the way the lyrics match them compels dancing, singing, and earned both songs a viral rating.

The same is true with writing, or that movie you may have seen a dozen times but can't stop watching. The words match the beat of the story well. The beat is just a different way to say the rhythm or timing of events.

For example, we said above that you need a hook right away and an inciting incident before the approximately the 12-15% mark of your novel. This timing involves "beats" the reader expects even though they may have no idea what they are called.

Those are the "big beats" or the large timing in your story, and they are all you need to worry about at the plotting stage. There are equally important and smaller scene beats, but if you focus on those consciously during the drafting phase, you will often kill the pacing of your story unintentionally. It is better to let your subconscious feel those, and then work on them in more detail when you are in the revision process.

There are a ton of books on this topic too. Some started in screenplays, like the *Save the Cat* method. There is a book that breaks down its application to novels called *Save the Cat Writes a Novel*, and I highly recommend it. But there are others: *Story Engineering*, *Million Dollar Outlines*, *Romancing the Beat*, *The Snowflake Method* (and a software that goes with it, Snowflake Pro). The last software is even free if you buy the book that goes with it, and you can import the files you create using it into Plottr.

The most important thing to remember is this: if you are going to use a tool like Plottr and a story structure template for your plot, you should at least understand the basics of that particular story structure, have a more general understanding of story overall, and also work to adopt them to a flow that works for you, your stories, and your characters.

A story has rhythm, and your interesting characters in an interesting place doing interesting things in interesting ways need to move through the beginning, middle, and end in time with the beats of your story.

The basics, those that are a part of any story structure, but sometimes called by different names, are as follows (arranged in a three act structure):

- **The Hook:** The event that draws the reader into your story.
- **The Inciting Incident:** The event that sets the hero on the path of a journey into a new world or adventure.
- **Plot Point One:** A change of direction, usually downward, resulting from a try/fail that happens just as we move from act one into act two.
- **The Midpoint:** This is the middle of your story, and is usually a big change of thinking process for your character that changes them from being reactive (reacting to what happens to them) to being proactive (taking action instead of reacting).

- **The Dark Night of the Soul:** The worst moment for your hero in the story, and one that turns them from despair and the worry that all is lost and hopelessness to the realization that they might just be able to win after all.
- **The Climax or Final Battle:** The moment your reader has been waiting for, and when your hero wins the final battle against the antagonist. This is the resolution of the story arc.
- **The Denouement:** The hero returns to the ordinary world we saw at the beginning of the story but changed because of what they have experienced. This is the resolution of the character arc.

There are additions to this, like pint points and specific try/fail moments. What's provided in this chapter is a high-level view of the essential major beats in the plotting process. Understand they exist and you can use different methods to guide your writing. You will want to dig deeper into story structure and major and minor beats, especially during the revision process.

By now you should have a pretty robust plot, with characters, places, events, and even an idea of where you are going and how you will get there.

Now you're going to take the next daring step, and summarize your story before you even get started.

7

SUMMARIZING YOUR PLOT THREE WAYS

"It's obvious man! We threw out a ringer for the ringer. There never was any money, man!"

-Walter

While writing a synopsis should be easy, writers absolutely loathe the process. It is akin to some kind of severe torture. However, it is essential, and if you write your synopsis first, you can reveal fatal flaws in your plot that can result in writer's block, a horrible draft, or worse, you not finishing your book at all.

I hear you. All of you. Sighing. Wanting to skip this chapter. Don't. Take a deep breath. Take a shot of your favorite beverage, adult or otherwise. If it's early where you are reading this, get some coffee first. Maybe a little extra. Let's get started.

THE THREE LITTLE SUMMARIES

Okay, so maybe they are not little. Well, not all of them. But there are at least three different summaries you should create for your book. You have probably heard of a couple of them. However, a deeper understanding will help you at the plotting stage.

- **The Elevator Pitch:** This is the one to two sentence summary of your book you will give when someone asks: "What is your book about?" **Warning:** If you cannot summarize your plot in one to two sentences, either you don't understand it well enough yet, or it is too complicated. Don't worry. We'll talk about how to do this.
- **The Sales Blurb:** This is the blurb you will use to sell your book. The reason I say three summaries is that there are three types, but you will probably have more than one sales blurb depending on the platform, length requirements, and other factors. We are only going to write one type during the plotting process, to keep things quick and simple, and you will probably change this once your book is written. In fact, I am almost certain you will, but having a framework now will help speed up that process later.
- **The Synopsis:** When an agent or a publisher asks you for the synopsis of your book, this is what they will be looking for. You will write out the various beats of your story chapter by chapter, and you will give away the ending. This synopsis will not be long, and the length requirements vary by genre. Again, the one you write when you are plotting and outlining will almost surely change by the time you are done with your first draft, but this will provide you with a place to start.

I know, some of you discovery writers just checked out, and I want you to check back in for just a moment. Sometimes writing the synopsis or summary first can help you develop even a loose outline. So stick with me. If by the end you don't find this useful, discard it. But you just might.

THE ELEVATOR PITCH

This is a really common thing writers are told to have, and that they hate. "How can I summarize my 300K epic fantasy novel or series in a few sentences?" You can, and not only that, you should, even if you are self-publishing and never plan to query an agent or editor. Why?

Because this will be the foundation for your outline and your other blurbs. This can be your novel tagline, another kind of summary we won't cover here, but one that can be a great help in marketing.

How do you do it? Take your original idea for your novel and add a few essential elements. The examples below are from my book, *The Call of Karen*, my NaNo project for 2020 that has since been published.

Step #1: State what your book is about in under 50 words, and turn that into a question, if possible.

Example: What if Cthulhu came to earth intending to cause havoc, and instead fell in love?

This is essentially the premise of the entire book, extremely simplified, as you shall see.

Step #2: Tell us the context or world of your story. Give us an idea of where and when it happens.

Example: Emerging from the waters of Delaware Bay, Cthulhu sees a beautifully angry woman named Karen arguing with a lighthouse manager about all the stairs. It's love at first sight.

Next, you will explain to the reader where the conflict will come from, and why they should care about your story.

Step #3: What is the conflict and why should the reader care?

Example: Cthulhu is being pursued by Kansas Smith, an earthly trophy hunter, and his archnemesis. He is joined by Gestalt, sent by the Elder Ones to return Cthulhu home. In this humorous tale of romance, flight, and pursuit, you'll find reasons to laugh and love.

Step #4: Pull it all together. It's time to put this into the few sentences that will wow an agent, editor, and reader, and get them to say the magic words: "Tell me more."

Example: What if Cthulhu came to earth for a vacation intending to create havoc, but instead fell in love? Emerging from the icy waters of Delaware Bay, Cthulhu sees Karen, a beautifully angry woman complaining to the lighthouse manager about all the stairs. It's love at first sight.

But Cthulhu is being pursued by an earthly treasure hunter, Kansas Smith, and Gestalt, an emissary of the Elder Ones. This humorous tale of romance, flight, and pursuit will give you reasons to both laugh and love.

Bam! You have a few sentence summary of your plot you can deliver in just a few short seconds. With any luck, it will grab the reader's attention. Note that this is the only blurb unlikely to change as you write your story: it is so high level that any deviations would result in major variations from the plot.

You can have these, certainly, but they should be unlikely. This summary should not go deep enough for that to happen.

For some discovery writers, you might be tempted to stop here. Don't. The next two summary types have things you can use too.

But even if you do stop here, at least you have a general overview of your story.

THE SALES BLURB

This blurb can be a little trickier at this point, but it can help guide you in your plotting if you construct it well. Remember, this does not have to be perfect. You're really selling yourself on the story and giving yourself some direction.

Here's how it goes:

- Introduce your main character and the hook to the story.
- Introduce your secondary character.
- Introduce the inciting incident and the main problem in your story.
- Ask a couple of questions about the solution that introduce stakes and conflict.
- Offer a few choices of what the outcome could be.

An example, *The Call of Karen* again:

Cthulhu escapes the underworld and heads to Delaware Bay for a vacation. Why Delaware? Because the mouth of the bay looks like it might swallow ships and he likes that. Emerging from the icy water, he spots Karen, a beautifully angry looking woman. She's complaining to the manager about all the stairs in the lighthouse, and Cthulhu falls in love with her angst. She's equally stricken by the watery presence of evil.

But before they can truly connect, Kansas Smith, an earthly treasure hunter shows up accompanied by Gestalt, sent by the Elder Ones to return Cthulhu to his rightful place in the Dark Realm. Recognizing the danger, they acquire transportation and flee the scene with Kansas not far behind. As they struggle to navigate their relationship among the shared hatred they have for pretty much anything, their pursuers get closer and closer.

Will the two of them escape into a love founded on shared angst? Or will Kansas catch them first, and wrest the treasure he seeks from the hands of evil? You won't know the answers until the final complaint has been filed with the manager.

Simple, rough, and inelegant, this gives me a path to follow, and a pretty compelling sales pitch as long as your name is not Karen or Cthulhu. If it is, I'm sorry in advance.

Now you have two general summaries, so it is time to get more specific.

THE SYNOPSIS

This is essentially a written summary of your outline, where you even give the ending away. I won't share my example here (spoiler alert) but I will give you a template to follow. Here you go:

Determine your premise. This is where your elevator pitch helps.

Reveal your story structure. Include things like:

- A riveting opener
- An inciting incident that changes everything
- A series of crises that build tension

- A climax where everything comes to a head and is resolved
- A satisfying ending

Flesh things out.

- Reveal the hook.
- Map out the story using the major beats.
- Reveal the main character, villain, and any other main character story arcs.

Some guides will tell you to reveal the beats chapter by chapter, but you don't have to. The point is to get the whole summary written out in word form, and to do it in under 1,000 words, preferably more than 500. The sweet spot is right between the two at 750 words.

Again, there are entire books and courses on writing a good synopsis. If you have time, read them, and follow their advice. If you don't, that's okay. You can do some learning as you go and flesh out your synopsis after the first draft is complete.

That's the key here. With some simple guidelines, you want to outline your story and plot it quickly, no matter what method you use to do so. Once you have your summaries ready, and your plot is developed, you are ready for the final step: setting up the writing plan that will take your plot or outline from concept to a work that is publishable or at least ready to submit.

Let's move on to this final piece right away.

8

A WRITING PLAN

"Yes. The Little Lebowski Urban Achievers. And proud we are of all of them."

-Brandt

One final step and you will be ready to start writing. There is a resource page on my website that listed in the final section of the book. It has several links to some of the tools I use and how I use them. Check back often as the page will grow and evolve.

Before you run off to look at pretty things I have created over on that page, stick around for some more words, and we'll see if a thousand of them or so can draw you a picture of this process.

Or something.

I digress, again, which my wife declares as my super-power. My super-power is actually being able to send an email that is supposed to have an attachment without the said attachment, forcing me to send a second email apologizing, and hopefully including the attachment. I am amazingly consistent at this, so don't challenge me.

Oops. There I go again.

Back at it. The first thing you need for your writing plan is a tool to write your story in, but one that will also let you see and reference your plot and all the work you have just done. There are a ton, so I will name just a few, and link to most of them on the resource page on my website. Ready?

WRITING TOOLS THAT PRESERVE YOUR PLOTTING WORK

This is something I'll just touch on, and I will also warn you not to Google this or take too much time on it. When you are between drafts and have some time, if that ever happens for you, is a good time to research and try new tools. Until then, I will list some common ones. I recommend you start with the one you are most comfortable and familiar with.

To accomplish that, my list will start simply and go from there.

- **Google Docs:** Free and getting more powerful all the time. You may have to use comments and some tricks to make your outline work in this one. But it can be done, and writers do it all the time.
- **Microsoft Word:** If you are a student or employed anywhere you write more than an email, or anywhere you use any kind of Microsoft Office products, you probably have access to this tool. If not, you can get a subscription model to Office 365 for little more than you pay for Amazon Prime.
- **Apple Pages:** A freebie with Apple products, this is an up and comer that also has some great ePub options.

And with Amazon recommending ePub uploads now, it could become an even more viable option going forward.

- **Scrivener:** My favorite, this has folders, notecards, and all kinds of tools to keep your writing straight. It is more complex and there is a learning curve, but you can master the basics quickly and dive deeper later.
- **Novel Factory:** A Scrivener rival, this one is a little easier to learn, has a web-based app, but is more expensive, especially if you are a Mac user, as there is no desktop app, so you have to use the subscription model.
- **iWriter, Freedom Writer, and Many More:** There are literally tons of writing programs out there. Well, maybe not literally. I mean, I didn't *weigh* them. But there are a lot, and every writer has their favorite. Most have free trials, so check those out before you buy if possible.

You will likely find one of these programs that suits your needs. If you don't, hop over to the resources page when you get there, and get in touch. I'll try to point you in the right direction.

THE ORDER YOU WRITE IN

Believe it or not, some people write their stories out of order, including end first, middle first, or random order depending on mood, and then the second draft pulls it all together. If you are one of the people who says quickly, "Yeah, I believe that," then you are probably one of the people who write out of order.

There are actually a lot of writers who do this. I am not one of them, and most of them are pretty strict outliners. I might try it someday, but likely not. If you are still early in your writing career and struggling to find your way, you might want to try this yourself. If you do, let me know how it goes.

This method does help with writer's block, as if you have already written a scene ahead, it does "feel" easier to aim for that outcome and get there. Whatever you decide, choose the order you will write your plot in before you jump in and get started.

THE WRITING APPOINTMENT

If you have heard me talk about writing for more than about 12 minutes, you have heard me talk about setting a writing appointment with yourself and keeping it. I just have two words for you.

Do it.

No matter what. Warn your family, spouse, pets, and wandering salespeople. Don't let anything get in the way of your writing appointment. It is the best way to ensure that you will write every single day.

Set both a time and a place and stick to it. If at first you have to move it around to fit your schedule, get your rhythm down and don't stop. You may get to a place where you don't have to write every day, or you want to take a day off from time to time, but start by developing the most extreme habit first, and relax if you feel you can.

This is a big part of plotting because you are going to plot out your writing schedule. Right? Right?

Again, do it.

DETERMINE YOUR WRITING PACE

Determine the pace at which you want to write your book and set goals accordingly. One page a day will get you a 365-page book in one year, 366 in a leap year. That's about 250 words or so a day, and about half an hour or less for an average writer.

I would, of course, encourage you to write much faster than that if you can. The faster you write your draft, the tighter it will be, and the less likely you will be to lose your way.

But I do caution you. Pace yourself realistically. Don't go overboard, as unrealistic goals can be discouraging. I recommend setting a timer or using a tea candle. Light it and write until it goes out. It's a great technique and can take the pressure of a timer away, which is not a bad thing.

Like any other goal, set a large, overall goal, and milestones daily, weekly, monthly, and more that you can reach. Set rewards for accomplishing what you have set out to do.

THE SAGGING MIDDLE

We already talked about this, right? Nope, we talked about the sagging middle in your novel, not in your writing process. Just like in your novel, if you don't have rewards for yourself along the way, your writing process may get arduous and slow in the middle. This is natural—in the beginning, you think you are embarking on writing the next great American Novel.

However, by the halfway mark, you may be doubting the value of your story and the writing process can get harder. You will have to find ways to motivate yourself through this part of the story.

The better your outline and the more you have figured out about your story, the better the middle will go for you. It will be less likely to sag, and your writing process will be less likely to slow down. However, if you get discouraged, here are some tips:

- **Go for a walk, bike ride, or hike.** Get outside, and away from your writing, but let your mind wander and work through your story on its own.
- **Exercise.** Can't get outside? Do some jumping jacks or something to get your blood moving, even yoga if that is your thing.
- **Write a short page, poem, or story related to your work in progress.** Essentially write anything else, just let your mind play in the story world.
- **Listen to music.** Some writers have playlists related to their work. Others prefer music without lyrics. Whatever your preference, just sit (don't write until you are ready) and relax your muse.
- **Draw, sculpt, or do some other kind of art.** Your "writing muscles" could just be tired. Let them recover, then get back at it.

The most important thing to know about writing is that there is more to writing than just typing and putting words together. There is your state of mind, thinking, working through plot, creating, and more.

Give yourself the freedom to "write without writing" but always, always come back to creating the words even if you don't get as many as you wanted that day.

GETTING TO THE END

The final push of your story is usually as exciting for you as it is for readers. You are nearing the climax, and you are racing toward the events of your story that will resolve anything else. There is only one important thing to remember about getting to the end.

This is a rough draft. If you fail to resolve something, if you leave a loose end, you can tie it up when you do your revisions. You can't revise what is not on the page, so get the words down. Then go back and do some rewriting and reworking before you let anyone else see or read your story. Give yourself space and the freedom to finish, even if you finish poorly.

However, even if you think you are finishing poorly when you go back and read your words later you will find that your mind and your muse did a pretty dang good job for you. Your major revisions will probably come earlier in the book, making changes that will help you and your reader get to this point smoothly.

There is no greater joy or pain than writing "The End" on your story. Both are equally true. When you finally do write those final two words, you might need some time off to recover, whether that is a few hours, days, or weeks. Be prepared for the emotional flood that will come, especially if this is your first completed draft. You will be overwhelmed, and that is okay.

PLAN A CELEBRATION OF THE END AS PART OF YOUR PLOTTING AND WRITING PROCESS.

Whew. We've talked about a lot in this book and covered some things really fast and not in deep detail. That's because this little guide is designed to getting your plot done quickly. There are a lot of books on parts of this guide that you can research and read on your own, and a more detailed course will follow.

But for now, let's wrap things up with a quick summary, and get you on the way to plotting swiftly, writing faster, and earning more.

FINAL THOUGHTS: WHAT SHOULD YOU DO NOW?

"Well, that about wraps 'er up. I was sorry to see Donnie go though."

-The Stranger

What should you do now? Pull all of the information you have here together. As we said from the start, you can use whatever tools you prefer to plot your story. That includes everything from my favorite, Plottr, to Scrivener, Word, or other programs. How they can be used will be illustrated on the resources page of my website, and that will be constantly updated, so check back often for new information.

But let's review. Your story needs some basic things. First, you need an interesting person (or group of people) in an interesting place doing interesting things in an interesting way. Your story needs a beginning, middle, and end, and you should have some idea of the pace the story will have when you start.

This is true even for discovery writers. Having a general idea of your story's path and pace before you start will keep you from getting stuck. All these things should be included in the ways you will summarize your story.

Finally, you need a writing plan in place, one that will take your plot from its current form to a story. If you are writing your work to sell it, this helps you write faster and earn more by having more work in the pipeline of the publication process. Even if you are just starting out and don't even know if you want to publish at all, the satisfaction of finishing may inspire you to write more stories and continue to perfect your craft.

That's all. So what you should do now is go, plot your novel if you have not done so already as you read through this guide, and keep writing. If you need help, feel free to reach out, and be sure to visit the resources page on my website below!

Happy Writing!

Plotting book resources page: https://troylambertwrites.com/pocket-guide-to-plotting-resources/

ABOUT THE AUTHOR

Troy Lambert is a full-time writer and author. Having written over two dozen mysteries and other novels, Troy is well-versed in story creation, and he knows what it takes to make a fictional story real! Troy's hobbies and pastimes (when he's able to break away from the computer) include hiking into the mountains of Southwest Idaho, fishing in a fast-rushing stream, and going for a drive where his mind can work on creating that perfect twist to the book he's currently writing. A native of Idaho Falls, Idaho, Troy and his wife live in Meridian, Idaho. You can find his other works, including his latest book, *Teaching Moments*, at troylambertwrites.com.

ALSO BY TROY LAMBERT

THE MAX BOUCHER SERIES:

Teaching Moments

Harvested

THE SAMUEL ELIJAH JOHNSON SERIES

Redemption

Temptation

Confession

MONSTER MARSHALS

Miner Inconveniences

Tilting at Windmills

NON-FICTION

The Tao of Trek

Writing as a Business: Production, Distribution, and Marketing

7 Steps to Plotting Your Novel Quickly

THE DOG COMPLEX

Stray Ally

www.ingramcontent.com/pod-product-compliance
Lightning Source LLC
Chambersburg PA
CBHW051242160726
47994CB00002B/987